English Romanesque Lead Sculpture

Map showing the distribution of lead fonts in England

English Romanesque Lead Sculpture

Lead fonts of the twelfth century

George Zarnecki

PH.D., F.S.A.

London — 1957

Alec Tiranti

Printed by Portland Press Ltd., W.1.

Acknowledgments

I owe a great debt of gratitude to many friends with whom I discussed the various problems involved in this little explored subject. In particular I wish to express my thanks to M. Jean Bony, Dr. C. R. Dodwell, Mr. Christopher Hohler, Dr. Peter Kidson, Mr. Peter Lasko, Dr. Otto Pächt and Professor Francis Wormald. Although I had much help and advice from them, the views expressed in this book are entirely my own and any criticisms should be directed against me alone. I wish to acknowledge my particular thanks to Mr. G. C. Dunning, who allowed me to reproduce in this book photographs of the Lindisfarne mould (figs. 79, 80) which he discovered. This is particularly generous for he himself intends to publish an article on this subject. To Dr. C. R Dodwell I owe a very special debt of gratitude; several of the photographs in this book (figs. 40, 43, 44, 56, 57, 59, 60, 65, 68-70, 76-78) are reproduced by his permission, for they were taken by us both in preparation for a topographical catalogue of Romanesque sculpture in England on which we are working. In that book each of the lead fonts will be dealt with in far greater detail than is possible in this essay.

Some years ago Professor F. Saxl began to collect, with his usual enthusiasm, photographs of lead fonts about which he intended to publish a book. Nobody was better qualified to do this than he and it is a great loss to scholarship that he was prevented from writing the book by his untimely death. The photographs, taken especially for him by Mr. O. Fein, were put at my disposal by the Warburg Institute. I wish to express my gratitude for this to Professor G. Bing and Mrs. Henri Frankfort. Mr. O. Fein's photographs are reproduced as figs. 5, 7, 21, 22, 24-27, 47-52, 54 and 55.

I am very grateful to Mr. Cecil Farthing for permission to reproduce photographs from the collection of the National Buildings Record (figs. 18-20, 28-31, 33, 35, 36, 45, 46, 73 and 75). Figs. 61-64, 66, 67, 71 and 72 are reproduced by permission of the Royal Library at the Hague; figs. 32, 34 and 41 by permission of the Trustees of the British Museum; fig. 17 by permission of the Fitzwilliam Museum, Cambridge; fig. 6 by permission of Corpus Christi College, Cambridge and fig. 37 by permission of the Archives Photographiques, Paris.

If the text of this book is at all readable it is due to the corrections of Miss Elizabeth Edmonds and Miss Ann Macfadyen. Last but not least my thanks are due to the staff of the Photographic Department of the Courtauld Institute for the care with which they prepared the prints from my negatives.

Contents

THERE can be little doubt that of all the artistic activities of the Middle Ages, the most highly esteemed was craftsmanship in the precious metals. Chronicles are full of enthusiastic descriptions of shrines, altars, images, jewels and ornaments made of gold and silver and enriched with precious stones. This admiration for metal objects is well illustrated by Suger, the celebrated Abbot of St. Denis. Writing on the work done under his administration,[1] he did not even mention the wonderful sculpture decoration of his abbey, which was to revolutionise European sculpture, but he gave a very detailed description of all the metal objects made on his orders, praising their beauty and their marvellous workmanship.

In England the fabulous richness of metal objects in churches was often mentioned by medieval writers and this is confirmed by the reports of their confiscation by the Commissioners of King Henry VIII. On the destruction of Becket's shrine at Canterbury alone, they took away twenty-six carts of gold and jewels.[2]

Few of these medieval treasures now survive. Of course, nothing can replace these shrines, reliquaries, images and altars, but the few objects that remain, even if they are made of less precious metals than gold and silver, may reflect the style and something of the beauty of those principal works of which medieval men were so proud.

English Romanesque lead fonts are comparatively little known even to historians of medieval art. They have been regarded as a curiosity and no attempt has been made to examine their style or to relate them to the development of English Romanesque art as a whole.[3] Such neglect is probably due to the belief that, because of the inferior

1

material from which they are made, lead fonts are of little artistic interest. This, however, is quite unjustified. Moreover, lead fonts form the largest single group of Romanesque metal church fittings in England, and they can supply more information about general trends in the development of metalwork in this country than more isolated objects, even if these are made from more precious materials.

Lead was, in medieval times, more widely used in England than on the Continent, for England was the principal lead-producing country. It is understandable that when Theophilus[4] described the methods of working in all possible metals, he mentioned lead only in connection with casting rods for stained glass windows and as a material through which silver sheets should be hammered, for in medieval Germany lead was rarely used for making decorative objects.

There are a few Romanesque lead fonts in France[5] and one of these was cast in the same workshop as a font preserved in England. The methods of casting and decorating French fonts are similar to those used in England and, moreover, all the Romanesque lead fonts in France are found either in Normandy or in regions immediately bordering it. It is impossible to say, on the basis of the surviving examples, whether the idea of making lead fonts originated in France or in England. On the whole, England's claim is strong, for all French examples date from the end of the Romanesque period, while some of the English fonts might be as early as the middle of the twelfth century. However, lead was only a substitute for other metals, harder but also more difficult to cast, such as bronze. It is probably true that English craftsmen, while making lead fonts, were imitating those finer techniques. The earliest bronze fonts were made in the Duchy of Lower Lorraine, then part of the German Empire. Lower Lorraine included most of what

2

is today Belgium, the part of north-eastern France round Cambrai, the region of the lower Rhine, with Cologne and Aachen and the southern part of Holland. Without doubt the finest of all Romanesque fonts is the bronze font in St. Bartholomew's Church at Liège made by Rainer of Huy **1, 2** between 1107 and 1118. Its technical virtuosity and artistic quality places it amongst the masterpieces of Romanesque art and no wonder it was imitated even as late as the thirteenth century. The bronze font from Tirlemond, made in 1149 and preserved in the Musée du Cinquantenaire in **3** Brussels is not of the same high standard, yet it is a work of great decorative merit.

It was probably from the region of Lower Lorraine and from examples like these bronze fonts, that both France and England took the idea of making fonts in metal, merely substituting lead for bronze. Thirty lead fonts survive in England and of this number, sixteen are Romanesque in style and date from the twelfth century. In addition to this, one other is known from a drawing, the font itself having been destroyed.[b] No doubt the surviving examples represent only a small proportion of the original number. Lead is easily damaged and many fonts were probably discarded for that reason; we have records of a few such cases. It is reasonable to suppose that in most cases several replicas of the same design were made, but with the exception of one group of six identical fonts, all the remaining ones are unique. This, in itself, shows what a small proportion they are of the original total.

We are very much in the dark about medieval methods of casting lead and about the craftsmen responsible for making the fonts. Was it the plumber who covered the roofs of buildings with lead who also cast fonts? A gilt lead open-work mount, probably decorating an altar, was found at

Whitby and shows craftsmanship of a very high order.[7]
On the whole it is more likely, however, that the artistic
objects in lead, like those in bronze, were the work of
goldsmiths.

Many English fonts were cast in flat sheets and then
bent and their edges welded together, the bottom being
added last of all. Some were cast in several sections and
even if welded very skilfully, the seams betray the method
used. The fonts which have no such seams have probably
been cast whole in a clay mould with a core inside. Today
lead is cast in sand or clay moulds and we can assume
that the same method was used in the twelfth century. A late
79, 80 twelfth century stone mould for casting lead openwork was
found recently at Lindisfarne and perhaps similar methods
could also have been used for casting solid objects.[8] Such a
method would put lead casting very close, from a technical
point of view, to carving in stone and to cutting seals.

Map The distribution of the surviving Romanesque lead fonts
in England does not give any indication of the possible
centres in which they were made. The only exception is a
group of fonts in Gloucestershire, made in one workshop
and distributed along the river Severn. The two fonts in
Sussex also came from one, probably local, workshop. There
are no lead fonts north of Lincolnshire and they seem to
have enjoyed a greater popularity in the southern part of
the country. Only one font, that in Dorchester Abbey, is
found in a place of some importance, the others are in
small parish churches. This, however, does not necessarily
mean that no lead fonts were ever used in cathedrals and
other big churches, for changes in taste affected those
churches more strongly and they had more means at their
disposal of satisfying them. Being also used more often and
thus more exposed to damage, lead fonts had less chance

4

of surviving there than in smaller churches and in more remote districts. The twelfth century lead font at Wareham is placed on a thirteenth century base. Perhaps we have here a case of a font discarded from a bigger church in the thirteenth century and removed to a small parish church.

Probably the earliest surviving lead font in England is at St. Peter's church, Walton-on-the-Hill in Surrey. According to local tradition, it came from the royal Manor House Chapel nearby. Unfortunately, the font is badly defaced but even in its present state something of its exquisite quality can be seen. The font was cast in one flat strip and the pattern was impressed with a block carved with four different figures seated under arcades. Originally, the block was probably impressed three times, making twelve arcades, but subsequently the font was crudely repaired and three complete arcades and a quarter of the fourth were removed. Under every second arcade there was originally a projecting object of circular section, perhaps an animal's head, soldered on to the border, and this masked the change in the pattern of the foliage decoration.

The figures seated on thrones are probably apostles, for their original number was twelve. The four figures of the block are in different poses and vary in the details of their draperies. In spite of the damage, they still retain the grace and beauty characteristic of that stage in the development of English Romanesque art when it came under Byzantine influences. On careful examination of the figures, the so-called 'damp fold' drapery can be seen on three of them and so attention is immediately turned to manuscript painting, for it was through that medium that this Byzantine method of modelling the human body was introduced into England. When comparing the illuminations of the Bible of Bury St. Edmunds (Corpus Christi College MS. 2), **6**

4, 5, 7
9-14
16

which is the finest example of this style, with the figures on the font, their relationship is obvious. The figures in both of them have dignity and elegance and the draperies are logically arranged in their relation to the bodies they cover and to the gestures of the figures. The ' damp folds ' are much less pronounced in the sculptures of the font than in the manuscript but this is logical too. In the Bury Bible, the ' damp fold ' was the principal means of giving the illusion of the volume of the body, while on the font the three-dimensional modelling of the figures made it possible largely to dispense with this and use it simply as a decorative enrichment. The foliage of the borders on the font and the fleshy scrolls of the spandrels also have very close analogies in the Bury Bible.

This Bible had a profound influence on manuscript decoration, wall-paintings and even stone sculpture. It is generally accepted that the Bury Bible is identical with the bible executed by Magister Hugo while Anselm was abbot of Bury (1121-1148). We know from documents that the same Hugo made the double bronze doors for the main doorway of the abbey, carved a Crucifixion group with the Virgin Mary and St. John the Evangelist for the choir and cast a bell.[9]

Judging by the illuminations of the Bury Bible, Hugo was an artist of extraordinary talent and his works in metal must have been no less splendid, for from his contemporaries we learn that ' as in his other works he surpassed everyone else, so in making of the doors he surpassed himself '. These doors were made *arte fusoria,* which presumably means cast work. It can be assumed that Magister Hugo's style as a metalworker was related to his style in painting and one can well imagine that his influence on English metalwork was no less considerable than it was on manuscript painting.

6

Casting large doors in bronze was a feat in itself and having been carried out by such a great artist as Hugo, must have made a great impression. There are no records, to our knowledge, of any other bronze doors made in the twelfth century in England.

Could the font at Walton-on-the-Hill be related to Hugo's metalworks, long since destroyed? This is a tantalising question which cannot be answered with any certainty. It is undeniable, however, that the style of the figures on the font originated from the Bury Bible. This style is also distantly related to another work associated with Bury Abbey, namely its seal, an exquisite work of the middle of the twelfth century. Is it not likely that a seal of such quality, dating from the period when Magister Hugo was at work at Bury, was made by Hugo himself? This is very probable. Of course, a small object like this seal, however precious in itself, is of no great help in assessing the style of Hugo's major works in metal, but it certainly does confirm our belief that the style of the font originated at Bury while Hugo was working there.

The date of the font at Walton-on-the-Hill is between 1150 and 1160, for it was about this time that the 'damp fold' style was adopted in painting and sculpture at Canterbury, Winchester, Sherborne, Durham and so many other centres. Because of the widespread popularity of this style, however, it is impossible to locate the region in which the font was made.

R. M. James, who first drew attention to Hugo's recorded metal-work, was of the opinion that Hugo was an Italian brought to England by Abbot Anselm, himself an Italian.[10] This supposition, judging by the style of the Bury Bible, must be rejected. Although several Romanesque bronze doors survive in Italy it was not the only country in which they were made. Bronze doors, many of which still exist, were made in Germany from Carolingian times onward. But it is not in Germany proper that Hugo probably learned his craft. The Bury Bible seems to have affinities with the art of the Duchy of Lower Lorraine,[11] and it is likely that Hugo received his training there. Although no bronze doors survive in this region, the Mosan style can be recognised in the beautiful bronze doors in Gniezno (Gnesen) in Poland.[12] If Hugo came to England from Lower Lorraine, he probably knew the font at Liège and it is quite possible that he cast not only bronze doors and bells, but also fonts and that the font at Walton-on-the-Hill was inspired by such a font made by him.

These are only conjectures, of course, but, as we shall see later on, the links with Mosan art can be shown to have existed in the case of some other English fonts, thus reinforcing the probability that the initial influence came from there.

18-22
24-27 The font in St. Mary's Church at Wareham in Dorset differs considerably from all the other lead fonts in England. While they are all cylindrical in shape this one is hexagonal, receding towards the bottom. This is an extremely rare form, the closest parallel being an eighth century stone font from the baptistery at Nin (Nona) and now in the Museo Archeologico in Venice.[13] That font derives its form from early Christian as for instance those at Aquileia and Pesaro. But even in Italy hexagonal fonts are rare, though other polygonal shapes, especially octagonal, were frequent.

The Wareham font was cast whole. Its decoration consists of a pair of arches on each side of the hexagon, with the figures of the apostles under each arcade. One figure can be identified as that of St. Peter. Only four different types of figures were used in making the mould, each being repeated three times. For instance the block which was impressed in the mould as St. Peter, was repeated twice but in each case 21, 22 a scroll replaces the key. Another figure with a scroll was twice used without any change, but the third time a book was added. The procedure in preparing the mould must have been roughly this. First a block with a pair of arcades was impressed in the six sides of the mould, providing the frames for the figures. Then four blocks, each carved with a differently posed figures, were impressed under the arcades in different combinations, so as to avoid having two identical figures next to each other. Small variations between the figures were then made directly in the clay mould. After casting, the cleaning up of the surface was undoubtedly necessary and the patterns were made on the capitals of the arcade. Every second column of the arcade rests on a base cast in the form of a lion's head, which is a feature common in Italian Romanesque architecture.

Although in its shape and one detail of its decoration, the Wareham font shows Italian influences, the scheme of the decoration applied to the font is based, like that of most English lead fonts, on models provided by metal shrines and altar-frontals. No English shrines and altar-frontals survive, but many of them must have been of the types which still exist on the Continent. Particularly important are the gilt altar-frontals in Scandinavian countries for they show many marks of English influence, and thus probably resemble their lost English prototypes. Some of these altar-frontals are decorated with seated or standing figures under arcades. The font at Wareham is particularly suggestive as an imitation of some such English model for the spandrels of its arcade are enriched with nail-heads. Nail-heads have no justification other than decorative on a solid metal object, and are obviously a faithful imitation of the method of fixing metal or other plaques to a wooden core.

The figure style of the Wareham font is characterized by plasticity and solidity of modelling. The figures are rather short, and their heads large, but they are executed with great skill and even a sense of monumentality. In this they bring to mind stone sculptures rather than metalwork. In fact the closest parallel to this treatment is found in the figure of St. John the Evangelist on the Crucifixion relief **23** at Barking Abbey in Essex, a work of about 1150.[14]

The date of the Wareham font, based on the figure style and the form of the capitals, should be placed about the middle of the twelfth century or a little later. The handsome stone base is a thirteenth century work.

28-31
33, 35
36 In the case of the six Gloucestershire fonts, the same block was used for making the impressions in the mould, although not in all cases in the same way. Four fonts, those at Frampton, Oxenhall, Siston and Tidenham are identical. In making them, the block of four arches was used three times, forming a continuous pattern of twelve arches. The font at Sandhurst has eleven arches and the one which was originally at Lancaut but is now in Gloucester Cathedral, only ten. It seems most likely that all these fonts were cast in flat strips.

The decoration of the block consisted of four arcades, two with figures and two with scrolls of foliage, placed alternately and a narrow strip of palmette pattern running above and below the arcades. In all these fonts the pattern on the bottom edge of the lower strip is not very clear, obviously the result of the process of casting the bottom of the fonts. This was presumably done by reversing the font, filling it with sand to the required height and pouring in hot lead. The impressions of the block in the mould vary slightly and as the relief, especially of the figures, is very low, in some cases the figures came out imperfectly, without haloes or even arms. The foliage, because it was modelled in a more prominent relief, came out better.

The two figures are probably apostles. They are seated, holding books in their left hands, and giving their blessing with their right. They differ in the details of their robes but have otherwise the very similar characteristic of grave majesty. The flatness of the modelling and the linear treatment of the folds relate them much more to enamels and manuscripts than to sculpture. A useful comparison can be made here with a group of enamels which, though strongly influenced by Mosan art, are attributed to England.[15]

However much the figure design of the Gloucestershire fonts owes to enamels, this cannot account for all its peculiarities. And here a seemingly insignificant detail gives us a useful clue on where to look for further sources. This is a small quatrefoil pattern placed on both knees of one figure and on one knee and the waist of another. Such a purely decorative motive is frequently found in Anglo-Saxon illuminations of the so-called Winchester School. It is used several times in the form of a rosette on the figures in the Benedictional of St. Aethelwold, but the most striking use of this enrichment appears in a Psalter written at Canterbury **32** (British Museum MS. Arundel 155). From our point of view, however, the most interesting manuscript with such a quatrefoil ornament is a Troper (British Museum, Cotton MS. Caligula A.14) dating from about 1040, for it is associated **34** with the west of England. It was probably made at Hereford, and at the end of the twelfth century at the latest, it belonged to a house of the Augustinian canons of St. Victor, possibly at Wigmore or Bristol.[16]

It has been generally accepted that this manuscript was influenced by Mosan art. The blending of Winchester and Mosan features found in it was probably not confined to this manuscript alone. Perhaps it is not without significance that at about the same time as the Troper was decorated, three bishops in the west of England were Lorrainers. The figure style of the Troper retained the exuberance of the Winchester illuminations and the fluttering draperies, but under Mosan influences the nervous strokes of pen or brush became solid, well defined and even angular.

Lorrainers continued to hold high church office in the west of England after the Conquest and well into the twelfth century, and they were probably responsible for the second phase of Mosan influence in that region. For it may well be that the enamels mentioned above originated in the west of England. There are certainly good reasons for assuming that the three famous enamel ciboria, also strongly influenced by Mosan art, as well as the enamel reliquary in the treasury of Troyes Cathedral and the enamel crosier in the Bargello in Florence, were all made in that part of the country. Dr. Hanns Swarzenski has pointed out the iconographic and stylistic relation between the sculptural decoration of Malmesbury Abbey and one of the ciboria which is said to have belonged to that abbey.[17] There is, moreover, a similar relation between the Troyes reliquary and the Bargello crosier on the one hand and two stone fonts, one at Stanton Fitz-warren in Wiltshire and another at Southrop in Gloucester-shire on the other.[18] When all this is taken into account, there is sufficient evidence to support a theory that there existed in the third quarter of the twelfth century a flourishing school of enamel work in the west of England.

The use of scrolls of foliage to fill in every second arcade of the Gloucestershire fonts is peculiar to this group and with one exception is not found on stone fonts. Amongst the lead fonts in France, there is one which has a very similar arrangement, although the foliage used is of a different character. This is the font at Berneuil near Amiens. Far more 39 interesting, however, is the only stone font in England on which there is an alternation of figure subjects and scrolls placed under arcades. This font is at Coleshill in Warwick- 38 shire and it is of interest not only because the design of the foliage is similar to that which decorates the Gloucestershire fonts, but also because the decoration of this font imitates a metal model. There are two details which support this suggestion. First, there are nail-heads carved on the spandrels of the arcades as at Wareham. Secondly, the scene of the Crucifixion carved on the Coleshill font is of a peculiar type, a round nimbus encircling the body of Christ. From the character of this nimbus we can guess that it was derived from a metal technique: the drilled holes in it were probably filled in with coloured pastes in imitation of enamels or precious stones set in metal. This nimbus not only shows that a metal model inspired the decoration of the font but also reveals the precise origin of the metal object used. The Crucifixion scene with the circular nimbus was a peculiarity of Mosan iconography.[19] It is found on several enamels but the most splendid example is in a Mosan stained glass window at Châlons-sur-Marne. However, this window is stylistically 37 connected (is almost identical, according to M. Louis Grodecki)[20] with the enamels of the portable altar from Stavelot in the Musée du Cinquantenaire in Brussels. In view of this evidence, it is fairly certain that the sculptor of the Coleshill font used a Mosan metalwork as his model. The scrolls of foliage under arcades give the impression of applied filigree very much enlarged, and that was, we can surmise, their origin. The resemblance of the motives of foliage scrolls

13

on the Coleshill font and on the lead fonts in Gloucestershire suggests a similar origin for both. This is all the more probable for the analysis of the Gloucestershire fonts has already revealed dependence on Mosan sources. Whether the immediate inspiration came from imported Mosan works or their English imitations made in the workshops of the west of England is more difficult to say. However, that the artist who cast them was an Englishman, there can be no doubt, for the arches and columns with their capitals and bases forming the arcades on the fonts are decorated with motives common in Anglo-Norman architecture. Moreover, while using a Mosan model, he retained some of the peculiarities of the local style, which had its roots in local Anglo-Saxon art.

In spite of these Anglo-Saxon elements in their decoration, everything points to a rather late date for those fonts. The enamels associated with the west of England date from the third quarter of the twelfth century and this was probably the period when the fonts were made. The distribution of the six fonts suggests that the river Severn was the means of their transport. The lead probably came from the mines in the Mendips and Bristol or Gloucester was the most likely centre of their manufacture.

One of the two lead fonts preserved in Kent was discovered in 1921 under a layer of plaster in St. Margaret's Church at **40, 43** Lower Halstow, near Sittingbourne in Kent. It was cast in five **44** identical sections and then welded. The ornament of each section consists of two arcades made of alternate plain and spiral columns, the plain ones being placed along the sides of each section, so that the welding does not show up too **42** much. The capitals of the arcade are of the enriched cushion type, well known in English architecture. They made their

14

appearance about 1130, but did not develop fully till after the middle of the century.

Under the arcades of this font are figures of a king and an angel. With the exception of the heads, the relief is very low for the legs of the figures quite disappeared in casting and only some traces of the feet are visible, resting on the cable moulding. The meaning of these figures is obscure, no other font, lead or stone, supplying any parallel to such a combination of subjects. The king is without a nimbus, but one must exclude the possibility of it being the image of the reigning monarch, for this would have been quite unprecedented. It can be said that the types of crown and the manner of wearing the mantle are similar to those on the seals of King Henry I and of King Stephen, but they can also be found on the ivory figure of one of the Magi in the Dorchester Museum in Dorset, dating from the second quarter of the twelfth century.[21] This little ivory figure has, however, no stylistic connection with the figures on the font. The elongation of both the figures of the king and the angel, the drawing rather than modelling of their folds, and above all the structure of the bodies with so characteristic a narrowing of the shape towards the feet, brings to mind the tenth and eleventh century drawings of the Winchester School and there can be little doubt that the inspiration for the figures on this font came from pre-Conquest art. Of course, in the process of transforming the pen-drawing technique into metal, the silhouettes became more solid and the lines of the folds have hardened.

The Lower Halstow font is not a work of high quality, yet it is not devoid of a certain naive charm. One must assume that it was cast by a craftsman of little artistic ability. He probably tried to copy a superior model, perhaps of an Anglo-Saxon date, which he obviously misunderstood. For

41

the angel he used looks as if it were taken from an Annunciation group while the king taken out of another context is here quite meaningless.

The lead font at Dorchester Abbey in Oxfordshire was the **45-52** only one made for a monastic house to survive the Reform- **54, 55** ation. It was cast whole with a strongly projected rim decorated with foliage and a similar band running round the base. Under every second column of the arcade this band is further enriched by roundels, which contain rosettes, interlaces, birds and even the Pisces of the Zodiac. Under the arcade of eleven arches are seated figures representing the apostles, of which five are repeated twice. As at Wareham, the figure of St. Peter is repeated twice, but while at Wareham a scroll was substituted for the key and this second figure represents an unidentifiable apostle, at Dorchester a sceptre **49** with a small cross has taken the place of the key and the second figure probably represents St. Andrew.

The treatment of the figures and the foliage shows a great richness of form and variety of detail. This is a work of an accomplished if exuberant craftsman. His modelling of the bodies is exquisite though some of the draperies create a rather over-emphatic surface pattern. However, one or two **50, 52** of the figures are treated with greater restraint and are of considerable artistic merit. They are reminiscent of the style **4, 5** exemplified by the font at Walton-on-the-Hill though they represent a later stage in the development of this style.

There is reason to believe that the Dorchester font was made in or near Dorchester. The figure style of the font **53** shows a close resemblance to the seal of Wallingford Priory, only four miles away. Moreover, in the immediate neighbourhood of Dorchester there are two almost identical early thirteenth century lead fonts (at Long Wittenham and Warborough)[22] and this suggests that somewhere in the vicinity there was a workshop specializing in making lead fonts.

Dorchester Abbey was re-founded in 1140 by Bishop Alexander of Lincoln.[23] It is reasonable to suppose that the font was not needed until the nave was built, at which time it would have been required for the use of the parish. Enough architectural detail of the original nave survives to enable us to date it to between 1170 and 1180. We can, therefore, assume that this was also the date of the font.

The best-known of all lead fonts in England is in St. Augustine's church at Brookland in Kent. Its general appeal lies in the attractive small scale representations of the signs of the Zodiac and the Labours of the Months. A great many fanciful interpretations have been given to the symbolical meaning of this decoration. Even such a sober writer as G. C. Druce has stated: ' That the Calendar appears on this font with a special significance is likely from the fact that there are three additional little castings just under the rim illustrating the Resurrection of Christ . . . The combination of this scene with the series of Zodiacs and Months appears to point to that favourite theme of the Early Christians, namely the lesson of the passage of time, the passing of this mortal life and the promise of a glorious resurrection and immortality.[24]

56, 59 60, 65 68-70

It is obvious, however, that these Resurrection plaques are stylistically later than the font. The thick rim of the font is a later addition providing a more solid base for the hinges of the font-cover. We know that the order to provide font-covers to prevent the use of hallowed water for magic was made in the Canterbury diocese by Archbishop Edmund Rich in 1236[25] and it was obviously soon after this date that the plaques were made.

Each block used in making the Brookland font consisted of two signs of the Zodiac above and the two corresponding

17

Labours below. On the depressed arches are inscriptions, those of the Zodiac in Latin and those of the Months in French. Six different blocks were made and four of these were used twice.

57   There is a very similar font in Normandy at Saint-Evroult-de-Montfort (Orne). This font is higher and so there are two condignations of the Labours of the Months and the Signs of the Zodiac placed above each other, the total number of Months being thirty-two. Each of the four groups of eight Months is separated by a figure of a saint standing under a pointed arch. This font is more elegant in its proportions and superior in its execution. Its late twelfth century stone base is original and is a great help in dating both fonts.

     The similarity between the two fonts has been known for a long time but whether they were made in England or on the Continent is a question which has never been fully examined.[26] After studying the evidence, it must be concluded that the fonts were almost certainly made on the Continent. On examining the representations of the Signs of the Zodiac and the Labours of the Months in English calendars and on English stone fonts and other carvings, it is obvious that, in spite of many parallels, there are no striking similarities. But on turning to the calendars of northern France, it is possible to find strong affinities, not simply with single representations but with the whole series. The affinity may be demonstrated by comparing the scenes on the fonts with the corresponding illustrations in a late twelfth century Psalter in the Royal Library at the Hague (MS. 76 F 13). On page after page both the Signs of the Zodiac and the Labours of the Months show a striking similarity to those on the lead fonts, which are, quite naturally, only a simplified version. Thus, the inescapable conclusion is that the Brookland font was imported from the Continent. This would have been

61-64
66, 67
71, 72

18

quite easy as Brookland is only about five miles from the ports of Rye and New Romney.

The latest of the Romanesque lead fonts with figure subjects is found in the lead producing district of Derbyshire and was thus probably made locally; it is in the church 73 of All Saints at Ashover. The font was cast whole with the use of a stone bowl as a core. The block for impressing in the mould consisted of two arcades with a turret in the spandrels and a standing figure under each arch. The figures standing on sloping bases and holding books have their heads slightly turned towards each other; they are clearly intended to represent the apostles. Along the base of the font is a band of highly stylized palmettes. The block has been impressed in the mould ten times thus producing the rather extraordinary number of twenty apostles.

The use of only two figures repeated so many times does not speak highly of the craftsman's inventiveness, nor their summary execution, of his skill. Stylistically the work belongs to the last stage in the development of Romanesque art and dates probably from about 1200.

All the fonts so far discussed rest on stone pillar-like bases of the simplest kind, with the exception of the base at Wareham which is, however, a later addition. It is, therefore, particularly unfortunate that the only lead font with a very elaborate stone base, in all probability contemporary with the font, at Burghill in Herefordshire, was accidentally almost 74 totally destroyed.[27] In the ensuing restoration only a band of foliage and the upper part of thirteen arches could be used and so it is not known what these arches contained. Under the corresponding arcade of thirteen arches on the stone base of this font Christ and the twelve apostles are carved. On stylistic grounds, this font can be attributed to the third quarter of the twelfth century.

The three remaining lead fonts of the Romanesque period in England are decorated with foliage motives only. One of 75 these is in St. Mary's church at Barnetby-le-Wold in Lincolnshire. It was cast in one flat strip and its decoration consists of two types of foliage pattern, placed in three horizontal zones. The two lower zones are identical, having the same pattern of foliage, its leaves pointing upwards, while the higher zone is decorated with a richer design of foliage, its leaves turned downwards.

The effect of this type of decoration, although repetitive, is most successful and the work is of very fine quality. The forms of the foliage used are frequently found in English manuscript illuminations, but it seems that it was equally popular in metalwork. For instance, very similar acanthus palmettes are profusely used on a Danish altar-frontal at Sahl (West Jutland) and this motive is attributed by Mr. Poul Norlund to English influence.[28] Also in stone sculpture palmettes of similar designs were occasionally used.

A particularly interesting parallel for the font at Barnetby-76 le-Wold is provided by the tomb-stone of Gundrada, the wife of the founder of Lewes Priory in Sussex. This tomb-stone was originally in the priory, but is now in the church of St. John the Baptist at Lewes. In this case the palmettes are placed in two zones and though they are joined by masks, the general effect is very similar to the font at Barnetby-le-Wold. The tomb-stone was probably made for the second dedication of Lewes Priory, between 1142 and 1147. The forms of the leaves on the font indicate a somewhat later date, probably between 1150 and 1160.

The last two examples of Romanesque lead fonts came from one workshop and are found in two neighbouring 77, 78 villages in Sussex, Edburton and Pyecombe. Their decoration, though very similar, is not identical. It consists of a projecting

20

rim and three horizontal zones of unequal height. The top one is enriched with arcading made of trefoiled arches while the middle has a scroll of conventional foliage. These were made with the use of the same or very similar blocks, carved with two arcades and a length of scroll. The design was so badly made that the scroll does not run in a continuous wavy line, but forms an ugly break in the pattern at each joint of the impression. The same also applies to the columns of the arcade. The lowest zones of the fonts are each decorated differently. The font at Pyecombe has a continuous arcade with foliage scrolls, while the Edburton font has two symmetrically arranged stems of foliage with trefoiled leaves, framed by columns. That both fonts were cast whole is indicated by their thick rims.

Both fonts date from the very end of the twelfth century for the trefoil leaf is an early form of the type called the 'stiff-leaf' which became so extraordinarily popular in the thirteenth century. These two fonts, as well as the nearly contemporary font at Ashover, illustrate the falling off in the quality of lead fonts as we approach the Gothic period. The thirteenth century witnessed a definite decline in the production of lead fonts both in England and France.

*   *   *

What general conclusions can be drawn from this examination of Romanesque lead fonts in England?

Technically these fonts show many similarities in the methods of casting. These methods were obviously well known and well tried in many parts of the country. In spite of marked differences between individual examples, most of these fonts show striking similarities in the composition of their decoration. The foliage borders and the arcades with figures were almost a rule. Compared with the amazing variety of stone fonts, lead fonts form a fairly homogeneous group. They have little connection with stone fonts, and then only with those which themselves have been influenced by metalwork.

Superficially, English lead fonts are monotonous, because there is comparatively little variety in the motives used for their decoration. However, within this self-imposed limitation, based on the long established methods of decorating shrines and ultimately going back to Early Christian sarcophagi, the variety is endless. Such a discriminating writer as Herr Georg Pudelko calls some of the English lead fonts 'unbelievably fine works'. The same author thinks that certain elements in the decoration of fonts in Westphalia were derived from English models and considers it possible that English lead fonts were imported there.[30]

Stylistic differences between individual fonts, even if they are roughly contemporary, suggest that there existed regional schools of metalwork, formed under different local and external traditions and influences. Of local traditions, that of the Winchester School was the strongest and its presence in such different works as the font at Lower Halstow and those in Gloucestershire, testifies to the vitality of the pre-Conquest style, a fact well known in other fields of Romanesque art.

The fonts at Wareham and Dorchester show a certain amount of interrelation with stone sculpture and the question arises whether metalwork affected the development of monumental sculpture or vice versa. There exist many indications that metalwork played an important part in the stylistic changes of stone sculpture. The influence of the works of Nicolas of Verdun on French sculpture is widely recognized as one of the chief factors in creating the 'classical' trend in the early Gothic style. The 'metalwork style' in some English Romanesque stone sculpture has often been mentioned by various writers though they were unable to point

22

to any concrete objects in metal as parallels. The lead fonts can provide some useful comparisons.

One cannot over-emphasize the importance of the influences on English lead fonts that came from Lower Lorraine. In fact, as it has been suggested, the initial idea of making metal fonts probably came from there. Whether Magister Hugo was instrumental in this will remain a matter for conjecture. If, in the south east of England, the influence from Lorraine at about 1150 was something new,[29] in the west part of the country, connections with Lorraine dated back to pre-Conquest times. It was there that a veritable 'Anglo-Mosan' school of metalwork came into being. The superb works of enamelling had their counterpart in lead fonts. Moreover, the existence of a local workshop producing lead fonts influenced by the Mosan style reinforces the probability that the enamels in question were actually of English workmanship.

Footnotes

1. E. Panofsky, *Abbot Suger*, Princeton 1946.

2. G. White (edit.), *The Cathedral Church of Canterbury*, London 1896, p. 13.

3. The most important publication on lead fonts is an article by G. C. Druce, *Lead fonts in England, with some reference to French examples* in JOURNAL OF THE BRITISH ARCHAEOLOGICAL ASSOCIATION, new series, vol. 39, 1934. Also useful are the following: W. R. Lethaby, *Leadwork old and ornamental*, 1893; A. F. Fryer, *Leaden fonts* in ARCHAEOLOGICAL JOURNAL, vol. 57, 1900, with supplements in vols. 63, 65 and 78; L. Weaver, *English lead fonts* in ARCHITECTURAL REVIEW, vol. 19, 1906; F. Bond, *Fonts and font covers,* London, New York and Toronto, 1908, Chapter VIII—Metal and other fonts, pp. 75-87; L. Weaver, *English leadwork,* London 1909.

4. *Diversarum artium schedula.* There is an English translation of the Latin text by R. Hendrie, London, 1847. A new translation is being prepared by Dr. C. R. Dodwell, to be published in the Nelson Series of Medieval Texts.

5. C. Enlart, *Manuel d'archéologie française,* vol. 1, Paris 1920, p. 887 lists the following twelfth century fonts: Espaubourg (Oise), Berneuil (Somme), Saint-Evroult-de-Montfort (Orne), Bourg-Achard (Eure).

6. RELIQUARY, new series, vol. 6, p. 109 and L. Weaver, *English leadwork,* p. 2, fig. 1. The font was destroyed in 1891.

7. G. Haseloff, *An Anglo-Saxon openwork mount from Whitby Abbey* in ANTIQUARIES JOURNAL, vol. 30, 1950, pp. 170 ff.

8. The discovery was made by Mr. G. C. Dunning to whom I am greatly indebted for permission to reproduce the mould.

9. M. R. James, *On the Abbey of S. Edmund at Bury,* Cambridge 1895, on the bible see p. 7, on the bronze door see p. 128, on the Crucifixion see p. 134, and on the bell see p. 199.

10. Ibid., p. 128.

11. There is an obvious and extremely close connection between the Bury Bible and the Bible from Ste. Marie de Parc, near Louvain, dating from 1148 (Brit. Mus., Add. MSS. 1488-90). Byzantine elements were already present in Mosan art of the early twelfth century, as is shown by the Liège font of Rainer of Huy and a breviary from Liège, dating from c. 1100. (K. H. Usener, *Das Breviar Clm.* 23261, *der bayerischen Staatsbibliothek und die Anfänge der romanischen Buchmalerei in Lüttich* in MUNCHNER JAHRBUCH D. BILD. KUNST, 1950, p. 85, pl. 22). For a general assessment of the art of Lorraine in the twelfth century see H. Swarzenski, *Monuments of Romanesque Art,* London 1954, p. 29-32.

12. P. Francastel, ' La porte de bronze de Gniezno ', in *L'Art Mosan,* ed. by F. Francastel, Paris 1953, pp. 203 ff. The term ' Mosan art ' is applied to the art of the Meuse valley, with such centres as Liège, Maastricht, Dinant.

13. G. Pudelko, *Romanische Taufsteine,* Berlin 1932, fig. 5.

14. G. Zarnecki, *Later English Romanesque sculpture,* 1140-1210, London 1954, p. 58, pls. 65 and 66.

15. M. Chamot, *English mediaeval enamels,* London 1930, pp. 6-10.

16. I owe this information to Mr. Christopher Hohler.

17. F. Saxl (edit. by H. Swarzenski), *English sculptures of the twelfth century,* London 1954, p. 63.

18. This has been pointed out to me by both Mme. Serge Gauthier and Mrs. Trenchard Cox.

19. J. de Borchgrave d'Altena, *Crucifixions romanes* in REVUE BELGE D'ARCHEOLOGIE ET D'HISTOIRE DE L'ART, 1933, pp. 62 ff., Pl. III. See also Swarzenski, *Monuments of Romanesque art,* Pl. 169, fig. 374; L. Grodecki, ' Quelques observations sur le vitrail au XIIe- siècle en Rhénanie et en France ' in *Memorial du voyage en Rhénanie de la Société Nationale des Antiquaires de France,* Paris 1953, p. 245.

20. L. Grodecki, *Vitraux de France du XIe au XVIe siècle,* 1953, p. 44.

21. E. Maclagan, *A twelfth-century ivory in the Dorset County Museum,* Dorchester, in ANTIQUARIES JOURNAL, vol. 4, 1924, pp. 209 ff.

22. Druce, op. cit., pp. 16-17, figs. 16 and 17.

23. W. Dugdale, *Monasticon Anglicanum,* vol. 6, part 1, London, 1830, p. 323.

24. Druce, op. cit., p. 12.

25. Bond, op. cit., p. 281.

26. Pudelko (op. cit., p. 34) emphatically attributes the Brookland font to France and dates it to the early twelfth century. Druce (op. cit., p. 14) is also rather inclined to think that both fonts were made in France. He dates the Saint Evrault-de-Montfort font to c. 1180 and places the Brookland one a little earlier.

27. The font was damaged by the fall of the tower, sometime before 1812; it was repaired in 1880 (Druce, op. cit., p. 15).

28. P. Norlund, *Gyldne Altre,* Copenhagen 1926, p. 244.

29. The importing into England of fonts, tomb-slabs and other ready-made objects from the Tournai region also began at about that time, c. 1150.

30. Pudelko, op. cit., p. 104.

Notes to Plates

1. **LIEGE, St. Bartholomew's;** bronze font. Circa 1110.

   This Mosan font, commissioned by Hellinus (1107-1118) for Notre-Dame-aux-Fonts, was cast by Rainer of Huy. The scene shown on the photograph is the Baptism of Christ. The oxen supporting the font are based on the biblical description of molten sea in the Temple of Solomon, cast in bronze by Hiram of Tyre. 'It stood upon twelve oxen' (I. Kings, 25); at Liège the oxen number only ten.

2. **LIEGE, St. Bartholomew's;** bronze font (detail).

   Detail showing two men about to be baptised by St. John the Baptist. The technical skill is superb and the treatment of the human figures shows a knowledge of classical models unparalleled in contemporary sculpture elsewhere in western Europe.

3. **BRUSSELS, Musée du Cinquantenaire;** bronze font font. Between 1150 and 1160.

   On the extreme right of Pl. 4 a crude join shows made in a workshop specializing in casting bells. Like most of the English lead fonts, it is decorated with figures placed under a continuous arcade. The motive of the supporting lions is of Italian origin. The stone base seems to have been re-cut, probably in the fourteenth century.

4-5. **WALTON-ON-THE-HILL (Surrey), St. Peter's;** lead font. Between 1150 and 1160.

   On the extreme right of Pl. 4 a crude join shows

where part of the arcading was cut away. The projections on the rim were made probably in the thirteenth century for fixing the font cover. Under every second figure some circular object was soldered on, which can be seen from the traces on the ornamental band. They were probably the heads of lions. The heads of all the figures are defaced, probably deliberately.

6. **CAMBRIDGE, Corpus Christi College;** Bury Bible (MS. 2, detail of folio 281v): Christ in Majesty. Before 1148.

This illumination by Magister Hugo shows well the use of the 'damp fold' drapery for the modelling of the human body. It is claimed in the text that Hugo received his training in the Duchy of Lower Lorraine.

7. **WALTON-ON-THE-HILL;** lead font (detail): an apostle.

The indebtedness of the style of this font to the Bury Bible cannot be fully shown by illustrating one detail only from the manuscript. However, even this one illustration (Pl. 6) is sufficient to demonstrate the close resemblance between the two works. The semicircular folds on the breast and the 'damp fold' falling diagonally across the legs are very similar in both cases. But it is the general treatment of the figures, their proportions and the graceful flow of the folds that speaks so convincingly in favour of the close dependence of the font on Hugo's style.

8. **BURY ST. EDMUND ABBEY (Suffolk);** Seal: St. Edmund enthroned. Circa 1150.

There is a strong probability that this seal was

made by Magister Hugo. In making the seal the older prototypes representing St. Edmund had to be followed and thus he sits on a throne that is more appropriate to the eleventh century than the twelfth. The cloak fastened on the shoulder is also a convention usual in the representation of a king (see Pl. 44). The figure is more elongated than in the Bury Bible, but it had to be fitted into the vesica-shaped form of the seal. The treatment of the figure is, however, characteristic of Hugo's style. The ' damp fold ' is seen across the breast of the saint.

9. **WALTON-ON-THE-HILL;** lead font (detail): an apostle.

There is a close similarity of style between this and other figures on the font and the Bury seal.

10–11. **WALTON-ON-THE-HILL;** lead font (details): apostles.

These are two further types of figures from the font. In spite of the defaced heads these figures must rank amongst the finest works of Romanesque sculpture in England.

12–13. **WALTON-ON-THE-HILL;** lead font (details).

The pattern on the bottom border changes between every second figure. It consists of thickly entwined stems of foliage.

14. **WALTON-ON-THE-HILL;** lead font (detail).

The ornamental border of the rim is enriched with a symmetrical pattern of leaves, repeated many times. The motive is derived from broad acanthus leaves, frequently used in the metalwork of Lower Lorraine.

15. **BERLIN, Museum;** Portable altar. Circa 1150.

This exquisite work by Eilbert of Cologne (it is signed ' Eilbertus Coloniensis me fecit ') is made of gilt copper and enamel. The ornament above and below the columns shows a marked similarity to the border of the font at Walton-on-the-Hill.

16. **WALTON-ON-THE-HILL;** lead font (detail).

The spandrels of the arches are decorated with four different designs of foliage. They are very similar to motives used in the Bury Bible and also in Mosan metalwork, thus once again pointing to Lower Lorraine as the source of Hugo's art.

17. **CAMBRIDGE, Fitzwilliam Museum;** Casket. Circa 1150.

This casket with an embossed silver and enamel decoration is the work of a Mosan artist. The foliage ornament in the spandrel bears a marked resemblance to the corresponding enrichment on the font at Walton-on-the-Hill.

18. **WAREHAM (Dorset), St. Mary's;** lead font. Circa 1150.

The hexagonal bowl is placed on a thirteenth century octagonal stone base. The unusual shape of the font is probably derived from Italian models.

19. **WAREHAM;** lead font.

Four different blocks were used for impressing the figures in the mould. On this photograph all four types are seen simultaneously.

20. **WAREHAM;** lead font.

Another view of the font, showing well the lion's heads supporting every second column of the arcade and the ornamental nail-heads in the spandrels.

21–22. **WAREHAM;** lead font.

The figure of St. Peter with the key on Pl. 21 and the central figure on Pl. 22 were made with the same block. The figure on Pl. 22 holds a scroll which was presumably made directly in the mould.

23. **BARKING ABBEY (Essex);** detail of rood: St. John. Circa 1150.

This is a detail from the Crucifixion relief, distantly related in style to the well-known Chichester reliefs. It is not suggested that there is any direct connection between this relief and the Wareham font, but merely that the figure style of the font has certain features that are characteristic of the contemporary style in stone sculpture.

24. **WAREHAM;** lead font (detail).

The presence of a stone relief in Dorset, carved by the master of the Chichester reliefs and the Dorset origin of the stone used for carving the Chichester reliefs suggests the possibility of a local, Dorset workshop responsible for both sets of works. The Barking rood is related stylistically to the Chichester reliefs. Thus the figure style of the Wareham font may well be connected with the contemporary stone sculpture of the region. (See G. Zarnecki, *The Chichester reliefs* in ARCHAEOLOGICAL JOURNAL, vol. 110, 1953, pp. 106-119).

25–27. **WAREHAM;** lead font (detail).

Although nearly contemporary with the font at Walton-on-the-Hill, and using a similar method of decoration, the style of the Wareham font is totally different. The figures are more massive, the modelling of the bodies more pronounced. It is clearly a case of two different artistic traditions.

28. **SISTON (Gloucestershire), St. Anne's;** lead font. Third quarter of the twelfth century.

One of the six identical fonts in Gloucestershire made with the use of the same blocks.

29. **FRAMPTON-ON-SEVERN (Gloucestershire), St. Mary's.** Third quarter of the twelfth century.

All the fonts of this group were cast in a flat strip, then bent and welded. The seam runs across a column of the arcade (centre of the photograph) and is fairly well concealed. This particular font has not been very successfully cast. The hands of the figures are for instance hardly visible. The next example (Pl. 30) was in this respect more successful.

30. **SISTON (Gloucestershire);** lead font. Third quarter of the twelfth century.

Anglo-Norman arcading, palmette borders, exquisite foliage scrolls under every second arcade alternating with the seated figures of the apostles, make up this rich decoration, unequalled in any other lead font.

31. **OXENHALL (Gloucestershire), St. Anne's;** lead font (detail).

One of the two types of figures used in decorating the fonts of this Gloucestershire group. Although inspired by Mosan metalwork, these figures retain something of the style of Anglo-Saxon art. The quatrefoil ornaments on the knees, for instance, occur also in the illuminations of the so-called Winchester school.

32. **LONDON, British Museum;** Psalter (Arundel MS. 155, detail of folio 133): St. Benedict. First half of the eleventh century.

This manuscript was written for Christ Church, Canterbury. The figure of St. Benedict is enriched by arbitrary quatrefoils. This method is rather foreign to manuscript illuminations and one wonders whether it was not borrowed from enamel-technique. If that were the case, the Gloucestershire craftsman could have used not manuscripts but enamels as his models, a far more likely possibility.

33. **SISTON;** lead font (detail).

The second type of figure used on the Gloucestershire fonts. Here the quatrefoils are placed differently to those on the previous example (Pl. 32).

34. **LONDON, British Museum;** Troper (Cotton MS. Caligula A. XIV. detail of folio 30v): St. Andrew. Circa 1040.

The miniatures of this Hereford manuscript are executed in the ' Winchester style ' modified by influences from Lower Lorraine. The angularity of the forms and their solidity is in contrast with the nervous, light, sketchy style of the pure ' Winchester ' works. That works of art in this style influenced the metalworker responsible for the Gloucestershire fonts is almost certain, especially in view of the Hereford origin of this manuscript. The quatrefoil on the knee of St. Andrew adds a further argument in support of this theory.

35. **FRAMPTON-ON-SEVERN;** lead font (detail): scroll under arcade. Third quarter of the twelfth century.

36. **SISTON;** lead font (detail): scroll under arcade.

Two blocks with foliage motives were used alternately with the figures. One design is shown on the previous plate, this one is from a different block.

37. **CHALONS-SUR-MARNE (Marne), Cathedral;** stained glass: Crucifixion. Circa 1155.

This Crucifixion within a circular nimbus closely resembles Mosan enamels in style and iconography and it has been proved by M. Louis Grodecki to be the work of a Mosan artist.

38. **COLESHILL (Warwickshire), St. Peter and St. Paul;** stone font. Between 1150 and 1160.

The foliage under arcades alternates with figures. It is suggested in the text that this peculiar arrangement found also on the Gloucestershire fonts, was derived from Mosan metalwork.

39. **BERNEUIL (Somme);** lead font. Third quarter of the twelfth century.

This font is decorated with a figure of St. Peter, repeated alternately with foliage. Another font made with the use of the same blocks, but having two more arches, is found at Espaubourg (Oise). The idea of placing figures and foliage in alternating order under arcades is very similar to that used in decorating the Gloucestershire fonts.

40. **LOWER HALSTOW (Kent), St. Margaret's;** lead font. Third quarter of the twelfth century.

This font was plastered over and was thus preserved from damage by the Puritans. Its decoration was revealed when plaster cracked as a result of the vibration from guns during the first world war. The font was skilfully repaired in 1921.

The capitals of the arcade decorating this font are of the type familiar from Anglo-Norman architecture. The linear treatment of the figures and especially the characteristic narrowing of their shapes towards the feet recalls the pre-Conquest ' Winchester ' style.

41. **LONDON, British Museum;** Psalter (Harley MS. 2904, detail of folio 3v): Virgin Mary. Last quarter of the tenth century.

This is a typical construction of the human figure in ' Winchester ' manuscripts with elongated proportions, a narrowing of the forms towards the feet and modelling achieved through nervous, sketchy strokes of the pen.

42. **WINCHESTER, Cathedral Museum;** capital. Circa 1160.

Capitals of a very similar design can be found in many parts of the country. The earliest and simplest examples date from about 1130 but the capitals having a more developed form, similar to those on the font, should be placed at about 1160.

43. **LOWER HALSTOW;** lead font (detail): an angel.

The gesture of the angel is peculiar to the scene of the Annunciation, but the figures in the neighbouring arcades are each of a king.

44. **LOWER HALSTOW;** lead font (detail): a king.

This is artistically the weaker of the two figures: the modelling of the arms is especially unsatisfactory. The king, in contrast to the figure of the angel, has no nimbus, so presumably he is not a saint.

45. **DORCHESTER (Oxfordshire), Abbey of St. Peter and St. Paul;** lead font. Between 1170 and 1180.

The system of decoration on this font is similar to the font at Walton-on-the-Hill, having the continuous arcade with the seated figures of the apostles and foliage borders above and below. What is, however, strikingly similar is the use of circular ornaments under every second column to mask the change in the design of the ornament on the border.

46. **DORCHESTER;** lead font (detail): an apostle.

Six different blocks with figures were impressed in the mould, five of them twice. This is one of the figures with a comparatively undamaged face. It is a highly successful work of High Romanesque art which can be compared to such stone sculpture as the apostles in the porch of Malmesbury Abbey.

47. **DORCHESTER;** lead font.

The thick rim of this font shows that it was cast whole, with a core inside.

48–52. **DORCHESTER;** lead font (details).

There is great variety in the treatment of individual figures. Some (for instance Pls. 48 and 51) suffer perhaps from the division of the draperies into too numerous folds for the sake of achieving a rich surface pattern. Others (for instance Pls. 50 and 52) are more restrained and far more successful. Two of the figures on the font can be identified as St. Peter with the key and St. Andrew (Pl. 49) with a cross.

53. **WALLINGFORD PRIORY (Berkshire);** Seal: Christ in Majesty. Circa 1170.

This seal shows such stylistic resemblance to the Dorchester font that it can be attributed to the same workshop. Of course, the small size of the seal demands a more summary treatment of detail.

54–55. **DORCHESTER;** lead font (details).

The ornamental borders of this font are made of foliage cast in high relief. When compared with the corresponding borders on the font at Walton-on-the Hill, they show particularly vividly the stylistic change that occured within approximately the twenty years that separate these two works. The comparatively flat relief of the earlier font has been replaced by one that is fully plastic. To achieve a high relief in lead is an intricate and very skilful process.

56. **BROOKLAND (Kent), St. Augustine's;** lead font. Circa 1200.

In the arcade of the upper zone are placed the Signs of the Zodiac with Latin inscriptions, while in the arcade of the lower zone are the Labours of the Months, which have French names. Each block consisted of two Signs of the Zodiac and two Labours of the Months. The impressions on the mould were made carelessly and there are large gaps between the designs of each block. The plaques with the Resurrection of Christ on the rim were added in the thirteenth century.

57. **SAINT-EVROULT-DE-MONTFORT (Orne);** lead font. Circa 1200.

This and the Brookland font (Pl. 56) are the products of one workshop. The blocks used for making this font are smaller and thus there were two separate blocks on top and two separate blocks below. The resulting shape of the font is more slender than at Brookland. The blocks used in making the two fonts were not identical, yet extremely similar. The execution also differs, the font in Normandy showing a more spirited modelling and a livelier composition. There are further differences. On the font at Saint-Evroult-de-Montfort each group of four blocks is separated from its neighbour by a large figure, filling the whole height of the font and placed under a pointed arch.

It is obvious that the blocks used for decorating this font were originally made for another purpose. This is shown by the semicircular shapes cut away in the bottom part of some blocks. It is most likely that the blocks were made for water cisterns or other vessels with pipes leading to or from them. It seems probable that the font in Normandy was executed first from re-used blocks. Then, some time later, perhaps when the original blocks were destroyed, another font was made with the use of the same pattern-book. The semi-circular forms at the bottom of some blocks were retained, but modified to form small arches under a few columns. At the same time the Latin names of the months were abandoned in favour of French.

58. **SOUVIGNY (Allier);** Stone Column. Second quarter of the twelfth century.

The full series of the Signs of the Zodiac and the Labours of the Months were seldom represented in English Romanesque art. In France, however, such representations were very popular in almost every part of the country. The octagonal column at Souvigny is carved with a particularly lively representation of the Signs of the Zodiac and the Labours of the Months. Only a fragment of the column survives with five scenes of the Labours.

59. **BROOKLAND;** lead font (detail).

The series of reliefs begins, following the Old Calendar, with March. The first sign of the Zodiac is the Ram but the craftsman preparing the block clearly did not know Latin, for instead of Aries he inscribed the sign as CAPRICORNUS. Below, under the inscription MARS is a man pruning a vine. The next pair is TAURUS with a bull below, and AVRIL with a woman holding branches or flowers.

60. **BROOKLAND;** lead font (detail).

GEMINI, the Twins, are above MAI, represented by a man on horseback and with a hawk on his wrist. The next pair is CANCER and JUIN (for June), with a man holding a scythe.

The derivation of all these representations on both fonts from calendar illustrations attached to Psalters is shown in the next four plates.

61–64. **THE HAGUE, Royal Library;** Psalter (MS. 76 F 13). Circa 1200.

Scenes from the calendar. Pl. 61. Gemini (folio 6). Pl. 62. Cancer (folio 7). Pl. 63. May. A knight with a hawk (folio 5v). Pl. 64. June. A man with a scythe (folio 7v).

The similarity of the representations in this manuscript to the scenes on the fonts suggests their common origin, which, as the manuscript suggests, was northern France.

65. **BROOKLAND;** lead font (detail).

The Signs of the Zodiac in this case are: LEO and VIRGO (the Lion and the Virgin) and the corresponding Months are JUILLET (July) and AUOUT

(August). The Labours of the Months show a man with a rake haymaking and a man cutting corn with a sickle.

66–67. **THE HAGUE, Royal Library;** Psalter.

Pl. 66 shows a man haymaking (folio 6v) and Pl. 67 a man cutting corn (folio 8v).

68. **BROOKLAND;** lead font (detail).

LIBRA (the Scales) and SCORPIO with their corresponding Months: SETENBRE (for September) and VITOVVRE (for October). The occupations for these two months are threshing and treading grapes.

69. **BROOKLAND;** lead font (detail).

AQUARIUS, the Water-carrier, is represented as a man pouring water out of a jug, below is JANVIER (for January) with two-faced Janus drinking and eating at the table. PISCES, the Fishes, corresponds with FEVRIER (for February). The scene below is of an old man warming his feet at a fire.

70. **BROOKLAND;** lead font (detail).

SAGITTARIUS (the Centaur) and CAPRICORNUS with NOVEMBRE and DECEMBR(E) (the D in this inscription is reversed). A man with a hooked stick for beating oaks and a pig feeding on the fallen acorns is the occupation for November; for December the illustrated occupation is killing a pig.

71–72. **THE HAGUE, Royal Library;** Psalter.

Scenes from the calendar. Pl. 71 A man feeding pigs (folio 11v). Pl. 72 A man killing a pig (folio 12v).

73. **ASHOVER (Derbyshire), All Saints;** lead font. Circa 1200.

The falling off in the quality of the fonts produced at the end of the Romanesque period is already visible here. The very fact that two figures were repeated ten times around the font shows a lack of inventiveness.

74. **BURGHILL (Herefordshire), St. Mary's;** lead font on carved stone base. Third quarter of the twelfth century.

Only the uppermost part of the font is original leadwork. The base is the only known instance of such a combination of stone and lead sculpture in one font.

75. **BARNETBY-LE-WOLD (Lincolnshire), St. Mary's;** lead font. Between 1150 and 1160.

This is the finest of the surviving English lead fonts decorated with foliage motives only. The design of the palmettes indicates a close relationship with manuscript illuminations. Some Scandinavian metal altar-frontals are decorated with similar foliage, which is considered to be of English inspiration.

76. **LEWES Sussex), St. John the Baptist, Southover;** tomb-stone of Gundrada (detail). Between 1142 and 1147.

This tomb-stone, originally in the Cluniac Priory of St. Pancras at Lewes, is made of stone which it has been impossible, so far, to identify. It has some of the characteristics of the black Tournai stone but it may well be from an English quarry. The decoration of this tomb-stone shows affinities with the art of Lower Lorraine but can also be paralleled by English works, such as manuscripts, stone sculpture and enamels. It seems likely that this motive was introduced into England from across the Channel but was soon firmly established in English art and developed here more fully than in its country of origin.

The palmettes on this tomb-stone show an early stage in their development, those at Barnetby-le-Wold are more advanced.

77. **PYECOMBE (Sussex), Parish Church;** lead font. Circa 1200.

The decline in the quality of lead fonts in the late twelfth century, noticeable at Ashover, is also clearly seen on this and the next example. The arcade, formerly used to provide frames for figures is retained but the figure subjects are abandoned in favour of foliage. This is mechanically repeated all round the font.

78. **EDBURTON (Sussex), St. Andrew's;** lead font. Circa 1200.

This font was made in the same workshop as the one at Pyecombe. It is probably a little later, for the foliage used is of the 'stiff-leaf' type, character-istic of the early Gothic period.

79–80. **LONDON, Ministry of Works;** fragment of a stone mould for lead openwork from Lindisfarne (Northumberland). Circa 1200.

The mould has only half a pattern hollowed out and two holes which were to be used as guides for the second half of the pattern. Stylistically, it is related to the Edburton font for it has the similar foliage of the transitional type of Romanesque into Gothic. Figure 80 shows a plasticine impression from it.

81. **LONDON, British Museum;** gilt lead openwork ornament from Whitby (Yorkshire). Circa 1200.

Another example of a transitional ornament of the type used at Edburton. In this case, however, the workmanship is much finer and the lead was gilt. Professor G. Haseloff (ANTIQUARIES JOURNAL, vol. 30, 1950, pp. 170 ff.) dates this mount, in my view erroneously, to the eighth century.

INDEX

1. LIEGE,
ST. BARTHO-
LOMEW'S—
bronze font.
Circa 1110

2. LIEGE, ST. BARTHOLOMEW'S—bronze font (detail)

3. BRUSSELS, MUSEE DU CINQUANTENAIRE—bronze font from
Tirlemont. *Dated* 1149

4. WALTON-
ON-THE-HILL
(SURREY),
ST. PETER'S
—lead font.
Between 1150
and 1160

5. WALTON-ON-THE-HILL
—lead font

6. CAMBRIDGE, CORPUS CHRISTI COLLEGE—Bury Bible (MS. 2, detail of folio 281v): Christ in Majesty. *Before* 1148

7. WALTON-ON-THE-HILL—lead font (detail): an apostle

8. BURY ST. EDMUND ABBEY (SUFFOLK)—seal: St. Edmund
enthroned. *Circa* 1150

9. WALTON-ON-THE-HILL—lead font (detail): an apostle

10. WALTON-ON-THE-HILL—lead font (detail): an apostle

11. WALTON-ON-THE-HILL—lead font (detail): an apostle

12-13. WALTON-ON-THE-HILL—lead font: details of the bottom border

14. WALTON-ON-THE-HILL—lead font: detail of the upper border

15. BERLIN, MUSEUM—portable altar. *Circa* 1150

16. WALTON-ON-THE-HILL—lead font: detail showing one of the spandrels

17. CAMBRIDGE, FITZWILLIAM MUSEUM—casket: *Circa* 1150

18. WAREHAM (DORSET), ST. MARY'S—lead font. *Circa* 1150

19-20. WAREHAM—lead font

21. WAREHAM—lead font: St. Peter and another apostle

22. WAREHAM—lead font (detail)

23. BARKING
ABBEY (ESSEX)—
detail of rood: St.
John the Evangelist
Circa 1150

24. WAREHAM—lead font (detail): an apostle

25. WAREHAM—lead font (detail): an apostle

26.   WAREHAM—lead font (detail): an apostle

27. WAREHAM—lead font (detail): an apostle

28. SISTON (GLOUCESTERSHIRE), ST. ANNE'S—lead font.
Third quarter of the twelfth century

29. FRAMPTON-ON-SEVERN (GLOUCESTERSHIRE) ST. MARY'S—lead font.
Third quarter of the twelfth century

30. SISTON—lead font

31. OXENHALL (GLOUCESTERSHIRE), ST. ANNE'S—lead font (detail).
Third quarter of the twelfth century

32. LONDON, BRITISH MUSEUM—Psalter (Arundel MS. 155, detail of folio 133): St. Benedict. *First half of the eleventh century*

33. SISTON—lead font (detail)

34. LONDON, BRITISH MUSEUM—Troper (Cotton MS.
Caligula A.xiv, detail of folio 30v): St. Andrew. *Circa* 1040

35. FRAMPTON-ON-SEVERN (GLOUCESTERSHIRE)—lead font (detail): scroll under arcade. *Third quarter of the twelfth century*

36. SISTON—lead font (detail): scroll under arcade

37. CHALONS-SUR-MARNE (MARNE), CATHEDRAL—stained glass:
Crucifixion. *Circa* 1155

38. COLESHILL (WARWICKSHIRE)—stone font: St. Peter and St. Paul.
Between 1150 *and* 1160

39. BERNEUIL
(SOMME) —
lead font
*Third quarter of
the twelfth century*

40. LOWER HALSTOW (KENT), ST. MARGARET'S—lead font
Third quarter of the twelfth century

42. WINCHESTER, CATHEDRAL MUSEUM—capital.
Circa 1160

41. LONDON, BRITISH MUSEUM—Psalter (Harley MS. 2904,
detail of folio 3v): Virgin Mary. *Last quarter of the tenth century*

43. LOWER HALSTOW—lead font (detail): an angel

44.   LOWER HALSTOW—lead font (detail): a king

45. DORCHESTER (OXFORDSHIRE), ABBEY OF ST. PETER
AND ST. PAUL—lead font. *Between 1170 and 1180*

46. DORCHESTER—
lead font

47. DORCHESTER—lead font (detail): an apostle

48. DORCHESTER—lead font (detail): an apostle

49. DORCHESTER—lead font (detail): an apostle (St. Andrew?)

50. DORCHESTER—lead font (detail): an apostle

51. DORCHESTER—lead font (detail): an apostle

52. DORCHESTER—lead font (detail): an apostle

53. WALLINGFORD PRIORY (BERKSHIRE)—
seal: Christ in Majesty. *Circa* 1170

54. DORCHESTER—lead font: detail of the upper border

55. DORCHESTER—lead font: detail of the bottom border

56. BROOKLAND
(KENT), ST.
AUGUSTINE'S—
lead font.
Circa 1200

57. SAINT-EVROULT-DE-MONTFORT (ORNE)—lead font. *Circa* 1200

58. SOUVIGNY
(ALLIER) —
stone column.
*Second quarter of
the twelfth century*

59.   BROOKLAND—lead font (detail)

60. BROOKLAND—lead font (detail)

61-64. THE HAGUE, ROYAL LIBRARY—Psalter (MS.76 F 13): scenes from the calendar. *Circa* 1200

65. BROOKLAND—lead font (detail)

66-67. THE HAGUE,
ROYAL LIBRARY—
Psalter—scenes
from the calendar

68. BROOKLAND—lead font (detail)

69. BROOKLAND—lead font (detail)

70. BROOKLAND—lead font (detail)

71-72. THE HAGUE,
ROYAL LIBRARY—
Psalter: scenes
from the calendar

73. ASHOVER (DERBYSHIRE), ALL SAINTS—lead font. *Circa* 1200

74. BURGHILL (HEREFORDSHIRE), ST. MARY'S—lead font
on carved stone base. *Third quarter of the twelfth century*

75. BARNETBY-
LE-WOLD
(LINCOLNSHIRE)—
lead font. *Between
1150 and 1160*

76. LEWES (SUSSEX), ST. JOHN THE BAPTIST, SOUTHOVER—tombstone of Gundrada (detail). *Circa* 1145

77. PYECOMBE
(SUSSEX), PARISH
CHURCH—lead
font. *Circa* 1200

78. EDBURTON
(SUSSEX),
ST. ANDREW'S—
lead font.
Circa 1200

79. LONDON, MINISTRY OF WORKS—fragment of a stone mould for
lead openwork from Lindisfarne (Northumberland). *Circa* 1200

80. Plasticine impression of the mould illustrated
on opposite page

81. LONDON, BRITISH MUSEUM—gilt lead openwork ornament
from Whitby (Yorkshire). *Circa* 1200